EDGE BOOKS™

SANITATION
INVESTIGATION

SEWERS AND THE RATS THAT LOVE THEM

The Disgusting Story Behind
Where It All Goes

by KELLY REGAN BARNHILL

Consultant:
Robert Janus
Planterra Management Ltd.
Victoria, British Columbia

Capstone
press®
Mankato, Minnesota

Edge Books are published by Capstone Press,
151 Good Counsel Drive, P.O. Box 669, Mankato, Minnesota 56002.
www.capstonepress.com

Library of Congress Cataloging-in-Publication Data
Barnhill, Kelly Regan.
    Sewers and the rats that love them: the disgusting story behind where it all
goes / by Kelly Regan Barnhill.
        p. cm. — (Edge books. Sanitation investigation)
    Includes bibliographical references and index.
    Summary: "Describes the current sewage treatment system and the history
of human sewage treatment" — Provided by publisher.
    ISBN-13: 978-1-4296-1998-1 (hardcover)
    ISBN-10: 1-4296-1998-8 (hardcover)
    1. Sewage — Purification — Juvenile literature. 2. Sewage — Purification —
History — Juvenile literature. 3. Sewerage — Juvenile literature. I. Title.
II. Series.
TD745.B285 2009
628.3 — dc22   2008000537

Editorial Credits
Mandy Robbins, editor; Alison Thiele, designer; Wanda Winch, photo researcher;
    Sarah L. Schuette, photo shoot direction; Marcy Morin, scheduler

Photo Credits
Alamy/Andrew Fox, 16; Barry Lewis, 17
Art Life Images/Anup Shah, 20
Capstone Press/Karon Dubke, 4, 11, 14, 22
Getty Images Inc./Minden Pictures/ZSSD, 7; National Geographic/James L.
    Stanfield, 29
The Image Works/Syracuse Newspapers/Suzanne Dunn, 25
iStockphoto/Frank Vinken, 8; Oleg Kozlov, 1
Mary Evans Picture Library, 13
Minden Pictures/Michael Durham, cover
Nature Picture Library/Warwick Sloss, 26
Photri MicroStock/J. Novak, 18–19
Shutterstock/clearviewstock, 6 (yellow hazard stripes on road); David Huntley
    (push pin), 5, 10, 24; Gilmanshin (grunge background element), all; Jason
    Salmon (mud background element), cover, all; Larisa Lofitskaya, 6
    (sheet of paper with torn edges)

1 2 3 4 5 6 13 12 11 10 09 08

TABLE OF CONTENTS

Chapter 1
GOTTA GO

The average person flushes the toilet six to eight times per day.

It happens to all of us. We're in the middle of watching a movie or eating dinner. Suddenly, we start to squirm. We have to, you know — go. Not a problem, right? We get up and go to the next room. We have a seat, do our business, flush, and walk out. Nothing to think about, right?

Every home in every city in the United States has a toilet. It's the law. Flushable toilets help keep our homes and cities clean. But have you ever wondered what happens after you flush? Have you ever wondered where all that stuff goes? And what happens to it when it gets there? What do we do with all that poo?

EDGE FACT:

The oldest sewer system in America was built in 1842 in Mohawk, New York.

SEWER GATORS

Have you heard the urban myth that alligators live in the New York sewers? According to legend, deep in the sewers under New York City lives a colony of alligators. Supposedly, the alligators are escaped pets that grew to freakish sizes. True story? Nope! Alligators need two things to survive: clean water and a warm climate. Life would be very difficult for them in a dirty city sewer in the middle of winter.

However, according to an article in *The New York Times*, some boys in Harlem did find a sewer-dwelling alligator in the 1930s. The boys were shoveling snow into an open manhole when they spotted the 6-foot- (2-meter-) long reptile. The boys lassoed the creature with a rope. According to the article, the alligator had escaped from a passing steamer ship headed to Florida. Somehow, it ended up in the sewer. Sadly, the alligator did not live long.

According to scientists,
sewers are too cold
and full of germs for
alligators to live there.

Chapter 2

HOW THE WORLD WAS POTTY TRAINED

Ancient Romans built public restrooms. Human waste plopped into the pipes of the Romans' sewer system.

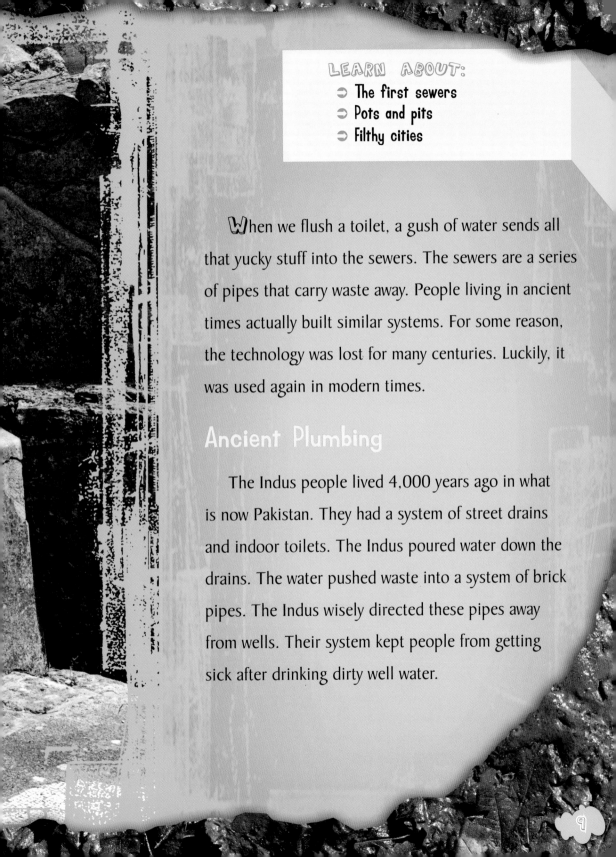

When we flush a toilet, a gush of water sends all that yucky stuff into the sewers. The sewers are a series of pipes that carry waste away. People living in ancient times actually built similar systems. For some reason, the technology was lost for many centuries. Luckily, it was used again in modern times.

Ancient Plumbing

The Indus people lived 4,000 years ago in what is now Pakistan. They had a system of street drains and indoor toilets. The Indus poured water down the drains. The water pushed waste into a system of brick pipes. The Indus wisely directed these pipes away from wells. Their system kept people from getting sick after drinking dirty well water.

Unfortunately, many later civilizations didn't continue using the Indus' intelligent plumbing inventions. Instead of toilets, people did their business in **chamber pots**. Instead of pipes, people had cesspools in their basements or backyards.

What's a cesspool? Picture a hole. Now fill that hole with human waste. Drop that nasty hole right in your backyard or underneath your house. You can even add garbage and rotting food to it. Yuck!

EDGE FACT:

The ancient Romans had a goddess of sewers named Cloacina. She had a statue, a shrine, and a feast day.

chamber pot — a pot in which people relieved themselves and then emptied

Some chamber pots had designs carved in them. Others had poems or pictures painted on them.

First Flushes

John Harrington invented the water closet in 1596. It was an early version of the flush toilet. But more than 200 years passed before the idea caught on. Most people saw no reason to bother installing a toilet. To them, it was easier to dump a chamber pot out the window. Plus, there was nowhere for the waste to go. Without sewers, it just ended up outside, flush or no flush.

As the cities in Europe and the United States grew, so did the number of cesspools. People even dumped human waste on the street. From there, rain washed it into the rivers. These were the same rivers people used for drinking water. They were the same rivers where people caught fish to eat.

Can you imagine those cities? They were smelly and messy. Wild pigs and rats roamed the streets at night. The animals ate much of the waste. But eventually, waste infected the water supply with germs. Terrible diseases killed thousands of people. It was time to do something. People needed sewers. By the late 1800s, many large U.S. cities had them.

Chapter 3

THE PIPES AND THE PLANT

Drainage pipes lead household waste through the wall to the stack, which is sometimes hidden behind a wall.

LEARN ABOUT:
- The stack
- Underground rivers
- Sewage sanitation

So where does it go? The bowl is full, you flush, and it disappears. It's magic, right? Wrong. As you wash your hands, your poo is just beginning its journey.

Down the Pipes

Go into the basement of your house or apartment building. You will probably see a tall pipe about 6 inches (15 centimeters) around. It's connected to your toilet. Plumbers call it the stack.

Flushable toilets use gravity and suction to remove waste and refill with water. Every toilet has a tank. It's the part on the back that's filled with water. You sit on the seat of the bowl. At the bottom of the bowl is a **siphon**. This pipe sucks out the water and whatever might be floating in it.

siphon — a bent tube through which liquid drains upward and then down to a lower level

Storm sewers and waste sewers are not connected. Rainwater usually flows into local waterways and is not treated.

When you flush, a gush of water forces the mess down out of the bowl. It travels through a pipe to the stack. At the stack, the water and waste flow straight down. The stack takes your waste to the sewer line.

The sewer line leads waste to the sewers under the street. Water won't flow uphill without being pumped, so the sewer lines flow downward. Wastewater from your toilet travels from skinny pipes to fat pipes. Each pipe goes lower and lower into the ground.

Eventually, every pipe in the city connects to the main sewer line. It is a large pipe deep underground. Some main sewer lines are just big enough for an adult to stand up in. Even bigger main lines have a wide stream in the middle and walkways on each side. The water flowing in the main sewer line holds the gunk from every sink and toilet in the city.

Sewer inspectors have the nasty job of examining sewer lines.

At the Plant

What happens to that gigantic underground stream of water, poop, and other nasty stuff? Before the late 1800s, wastewater was dumped directly back into rivers. People thought rivers would clean out the waste. They were wrong. People in towns downriver from big cities started getting sick. It became obvious that wastewater needed to be cleaned before it could go back into a river. Today, wastewater is cleaned at treatment plants.

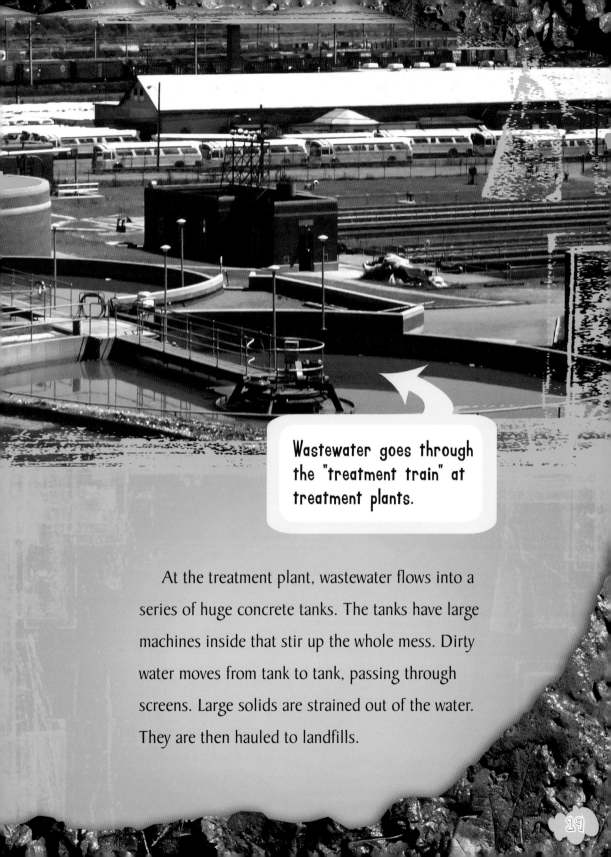

Wastewater goes through the "treatment train" at treatment plants.

At the treatment plant, wastewater flows into a series of huge concrete tanks. The tanks have large machines inside that stir up the whole mess. Dirty water moves from tank to tank, passing through screens. Large solids are strained out of the water. They are then hauled to landfills.

If untreated water is released into waterways, animals can drink it and die.

The water now has fewer chunks in it. But it's still filled with poop, poisonous gases, and germs. These things pollute rivers and can harm people and animals. At this point, workers add oxygen and special bacteria to the wastewater. Oxygen makes the **bacteria** grow really fast. As the bacteria grow, they eat the nasty stuff. When the bacteria run out of food, they die. The water left behind is a lot cleaner than it was before.

Wastewater then passes through two more filters. One uses sand and the other uses charcoal. These filters help remove any remaining germs.

bacteria — tiny organisms living all around us; some bacteria are useful, but some cause diseases.

Finally, the water begins a process called **lagooning**. The water is pumped into large ponds. Any remaining solid waste settles to the bottom, leaving clean water on top. Many cities grow plants in the lagoons. Plants eat even more bad bacteria.

As the water is pumped into these ponds, it is **disinfected**. Some cities use chlorine, the same chemical that cleans swimming pools. Unfortunately, chlorine causes cancer in some animals. Many animals may drink treated water once it is released back into lakes and rivers. Because of this, many cities now use ultraviolet light to disinfect water.

lagooning — a process during which wastewater sits in artificial ponds, allowing solid waste to sink to the bottom

disinfect — to kill germs

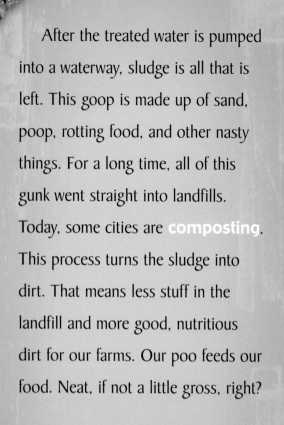

After the treated water is pumped into a waterway, sludge is all that is left. This goop is made up of sand, poop, rotting food, and other nasty things. For a long time, all of this gunk went straight into landfills. Today, some cities are **composting**. This process turns the sludge into dirt. That means less stuff in the landfill and more good, nutritious dirt for our farms. Our poo feeds our food. Neat, if not a little gross, right?

EDGE FACT:

Some people make their own compost. Egg shells, coffee grounds, and grass clippings can all be composted.

compost — to convert rotted plants, manure, and other wastes into fertilizer

At first, compost looks nasty. But later it makes excellent fertilizer.

Chapter 4

ENTER THE RAT

You may not see them, but rats live all around us.

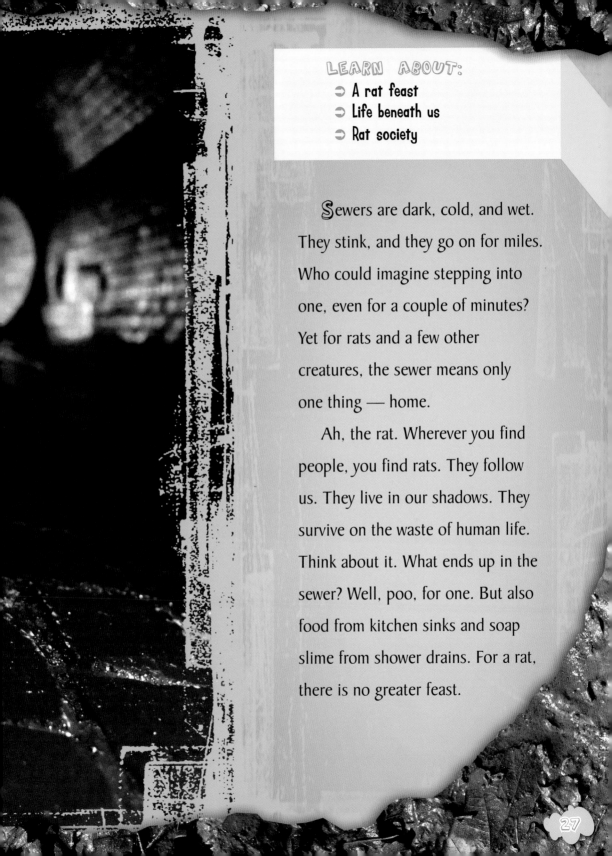

Sewers are dark, cold, and wet. They stink, and they go on for miles. Who could imagine stepping into one, even for a couple of minutes? Yet for rats and a few other creatures, the sewer means only one thing — home.

Ah, the rat. Wherever you find people, you find rats. They follow us. They live in our shadows. They survive on the waste of human life. Think about it. What ends up in the sewer? Well, poo, for one. But also food from kitchen sinks and soap slime from shower drains. For a rat, there is no greater feast.

The maze of sewer lines beneath us has captured people's imaginations for years. Legends are told of monsters and other creepy creatures living below us. In truth, we have rats, cockroaches, and lots of other bugs living in our sewers. Sometimes lizards or frogs make their way into the sewers, but they don't live long. There are too many germs and poisons there for them to survive.

The rat, on the other hand, is tough. Rats only live for about three years. But they pack a lot of life into those three years. They have lots of babies. They form communities and even make war with one another. Rats can't see very well, but their senses of touch, smell, and hearing are excellent. They are perfectly suited to life in the darkness underground.

Thankfully, most people no longer have to live side by side with their waste. The sewers are nasty, dirty, and full of rats, but they make our world a much cleaner place to live.

GLOSSARY

bacteria (bak-TIHR-ee-uh) — microscopic living things that exist all around you and inside you; many bacteria are useful, but some cause diseases.

cesspool (SESS-pool) — a pit that holds human waste and other garbage

chamber pot (CHAYM-buhr POT) — a pot in which people relieve themselves and then empty

compost (KOM-pohst) — to convert rotted plants, manure, and other wastes into fertilizer

disinfect (dis-in-FEKT) — to use chemicals to kill germs

gravity (GRAV-uh-tee) — the force that pulls people and objects down toward the earth

lagooning (luh-GOON-ing) — a process during which wastewater sits in artificial ponds, allowing solid waste to sink to the bottom

siphon (SYE-fuhn) — a bent tube through which liquid drains upward and then down to a lower level

suction (SUHK-shuhn) — the act of drawing air out of a space to create a vacuum, causing the surrounding air or liquid to be sucked into the empty space

READ MORE

Harper, Joel. *All the Way to the Ocean.* Claremont, Cal.: Freedom Three, 2006.

Huggins-Cooper, Lynn. *Water.* First-Hand Science. North Mankato, Minn.: Smart Apple Media, 2005.

Rosenberg, Pam. *Yikes! Icky, Sticky, Gross Stuff Underwater.* Icky, Sticky, Gross-Out Books. Mankato, Minn.: Child's World, 2008.

INTERNET SITES

FactHound offers a safe, fun way to find Internet sites related to this book. All of the sites on FactHound have been researched by our staff.

Here's how:
1. Visit *www.facthound.com*
2. Choose your grade level.
3. Type in this book ID **1429619988** for age-appropriate sites. You may also browse subjects by clicking on letters, or by clicking on pictures and words.
4. Click on the **Fetch It** button.

FactHound will fetch the best sites for you!

INDEX